BUDDHISM FOR BEGINNERS

A GUIDE TO BUDDHIST TEACHINGS, MEDITATION, MINDFULNESS, AND INNER PEACE

GABRIEL SHAW

INTRODUCTION

"Thousands of candles can be lit from a single candle, and the life of the candle will not be shortened. Happiness never decreases by being shared." – **The Buddha**

I would like to take a few minutes to thank you for purchasing this book and introduce you to what it will cover.

This book is an introduction to help you gain an understanding of the life of the Buddha and the teachings and practices within Buddhism.

The aim is not to convert you to Buddhism; many parts of Buddhism can be seen as nonreligious and more as a set of philosophies about how to treat living beings, with practices to incorporate into your daily life, such as meditation and mindfulness.

This is a beginner's guide but includes quotes and resources to guide you towards more advanced Buddhist teachings and writings if you wish to develop your own study of Buddhism further.

While this book is short, you should not rush through or try to finish it quickly.

We live very busy lives, and you may be reading this on the way to work, on a train or bus (hopefully not while driving a car), or you may be on your computer, trying to read this book while you are doing other things.

This book covers mindfulness, and you can incorporate mindful practices when reading this book by not being distracted by Facebook, emails, TV, notifications, radio, conversations, or browsing the internet while reading.

You can practice mindful reading by taking the time to sit in a quiet space inside or in nature and read.

If you are on a train or feel you don't have the time to sit and read this book, then you can just be mindful not to change between apps or websites while reading, focusing on reading it in your head, concentrating on each sentence and trying not to let your mind wander to other thoughts while reading.

Thank you again for your purchase, and I hope you enjoy reading this and learn something from it.

"Do not dwell in the past, do not dream of the future, concentrate the mind on the present moment." – **The Buddha**

1

INTRODUCTION TO BUDDHISM

Is Buddhism a religion or philosophy?

"My religion is very simple. My religion is kindness."
– The Dalai Lama

"However many holy words you read, however many you speak, what good will they do you if you do not act upon them?"
– The Buddha

WHILE BUDDHISM IS CONSIDERED A RELIGION, its beliefs and practices differentiate it from other religions, and it is often seen more like a set of philosophies than a religion.

You can follow the teaching and practices of Buddhism and still follow and practice the teachings of other religions. There are many Buddhist Christians that also follow the teaching of Jesus and celebrate Christmas and other Christian festivals.

Likewise, there are also many Buddhist atheists that don't believe in a spiritual deity but follow the practices of Buddhism.

*"Better than worshipping gods is obedience to the laws of righteousness." – **The Buddha***

Buddhism doesn't fit directly into a category like many other religions. The Buddha stated he just taught "the way things are," and his followers should not blindly believe his teachings purely on faith. The Buddha encourages each person to examine each teaching for themselves to see if they are true.

The Buddha understood that as science, knowledge, and wisdom progress, the teachings must be tested again against this new knowledge to see if they still hold true.

Some teachings and practices have been proven to be relevant today, as science can verify with studies and brain scans the benefits of practices such as meditation and gratitude.

Practices such as these are also especially applicable in today's hectic modern society, where people are stressed, distracted, unable to focus, calm their thoughts, relax, or take time to themselves to be present in the moment and calm.

Buddhism also isn't a religion in the sense that it doesn't require worship or obedience to an almighty powerful deity that controls the universe and the afterlife or who will punish you for your wrongdoings. The Buddha does not guarantee or promise an afterlife, as we might be familiar with; the Buddha is simply an instructor or teacher.

People may think, if there is no all-powerful God or deity, then there is no reward or punishment for being good or bad. Buddhism teaches that you will not be punished FOR your bad actions, but you will be punished BY your bad actions. We will go into this in more detail later in the book in karma and other teachings.

"No one saves us but ourselves. No one can and no one may. We ourselves must walk the path." – ***The Buddha***

There are many variations of Buddhism that would be considered a religion, some variations involving supernatural beliefs. There are also hundreds of millions of people in the world who consider Buddhism to be their religion.

However, at the core of the teachings of Buddhism are principles that anyone can practice, regardless of whether they are religious; for example, not harming other living beings; being aware and mindful of both your thoughts and your actions; striving for understanding; and seeking wisdom and living a moral life.

The Buddha also taught that you should question, obtain knowledge, and always seek the truth aligned with principles of the philosophy. The Buddha wants you to seek the truth, just as he did.

"There are only two mistakes one can make along the road to truth; not going all the way, and not starting." – ***The Buddha***

History of Buddhism

"Peace comes from within. Do not seek it without."
  – The Buddha

Buddhism is one of the oldest 'religions' still practiced in the world. It is over 2,500 years old, and its origins can be traced back to the fifth century BC to areas now within Nepal and India.

Life of the Buddha

Siddhartha Gautama (the Buddha) was born in 563 BC into a royal family in Lumbini, which is today located in Nepal.

In fifth-century ancient India, in the kingdom of Kapilvastu, present-day Nepal, there lived a king called Suddhodana, leader of the Sakya race, and his wife Maya Maha. They conceived and birthed a son whom they named Siddhartha Gautama.

On the day she conceived, Maya said she had a strange dream. In the dream, she saw a white elephant climbing a golden mountain and then a silver one that came towards her carrying a white lotus in its trunk.

The elephant touched her on the right side and dissolved into her womb. When the time came for her to deliver, Maya started the journey back to her father's land, as was tradition. Before she arrived, her baby boy came. She could not make it back to the land of her father to give birth, so she gave birth under a sal tree.

The king was elated; this child was like a dream come true and was named Siddhartha. He was a royal child and would one day be the king of his father's empire. The king needed to know the future of his son and his empire, so he called a Brahmin seer (Hindu priest) to predict the life of the young prince. The seer concluded the child would become either a great king or a great religious teacher.

The king wanted the boy to assume his rightful role as a king. He did not want his son to live the miserable life of a religious teacher, where he had to denounce his worldly possessions, his royal life, and title.

Secluded Life

The priest warned the king that, if the child ever experienced or saw human pain and desolation, he would feel compelled to follow the path of spiritual awareness. The king, protective of his son, raised his son in seclusion within the palace.

Secluded within the high walls of the palace, Siddhartha had no chance to see the outside world. His father made sure the boy had all the luxuries fit for a prince; he used material comforts to blind his son to the realities of the world. At the age of sixteen, Siddhartha married and had a son.

Exposure to the World

At the age of twenty-nine, Siddhartha secretly ventured outside the palace, where he finally saw the suffering of humanity that his father had been shielding him from.

He saw the cruelty of aging in the face of an aged person, poverty in a sick person, and death in a decaying corpse. The suffering he saw haunted him, and he could no longer find peace even in the palace.

Siddhartha had lost the innocence of not knowing any pain and suffering. He became restless and always seemed deep in thought. He no longer found pleasure in the material possessions provided to him. He constantly thought about how to escape the suffering he had seen.

When he went outside the palace again, he saw a spiritual man who looked peaceful and radiant. The man seemed at peace and was one with life. This intrigued the prince and prompted him to find out how someone could be peaceful in a world full of suffering.

Escape from the Palace

The prince decided to give up his luxurious life and material possessions and follow a spiritual path to find the peace he was looking for. At night, covered by darkness, Siddhartha snuck out of his father's palace on horseback. After escaping from the palace, Siddhartha followed a group of religious men.

This group sought enlightenment through discipline and deprivation of worldly pleasures, including food. They practiced extreme fasting. Siddhartha did this for six years, until one day, as he was bathing in the river, he collapsed and almost drowned due to hunger.

A girl nearby rescued him, gave him some food, and he recovered. That was his turning point, and Siddhartha left this life of deprivation and hardship and sought other paths to enlightenment.

The Enlightenment of Siddhartha

Siddhartha Gautama discovered the Middle Way and pursued this path of neither luxury nor poverty. He then recalled a day in his childhood when he had felt his mind settle into a deep state of peace. He realized any path to enlightenment would come from the mind and require a disciplined mind and meditation.

He sat under a sacred Bodhi tree and went into deep meditation. During this deep meditation, he was confronted by Mara, a demon representing earthly passions. Siddhartha resisted all the temptations and efforts to distract him and defeated this demon. Through deep meditation, discipline of his mind, and resisting temptations, he achieved enlightenment and became the Buddha.

Spreading the Teachings

After he reached enlightenment, Siddhartha left his place of meditation and went to teach others what he had learned. He encouraged people to follow the Middle Way, and he gave his first sermon.

In his first sermon, he taught the Four Noble Truths and other teachings, known as the Dhammacakkappavattana Sutta, still taught and practiced today by Buddhists.

In the years to follow, Siddhartha gained popularity as a religious teacher; as people listened to his teachings, his followers increased. He spent forty-five years traversing northeastern India, spreading his teachings. He reconciled with his father, his wife became a nun and disciple, and his son became a monk.

The rest of the life of the Buddha was spent teaching the principles of Buddhism. He continued teaching until he passed away at the age of eighty. There are many statues in Buddhist countries of the "reclining Buddha" depicting him lying down on his side, still teaching from his bed until his last day of life.

2

BUDDHIST PHILOSOPHIES AND TEACHINGS

"Letting go gives us freedom, and freedom is the only condition for happiness. If, in our heart, we still cling to anything—anger, anxiety, or possessions—we cannot be free." – **Thich Nhat Hanh**

THE BUDDHA'S experience after leaving the palace and encountering sickness and death had a big influence on his teachings. Suffering and how to escape suffering became core to the teachings of the Buddha.

The Buddha spent his life journeying around India, teaching others what he had come to understand about suffering, its causes, and how to be free from suffering.

Some important main concepts of Buddhism are:

- The Four Noble Truths
- The Eightfold Path
- Karma
- The Cycle of Rebirth

- Samsara

While there are more advanced teachings in Buddhism, these will provide a good introduction to understanding Buddhism.

The Four Noble Truths

The Four Noble Truths are the basis of the Buddha's teachings.

The Four Noble Truths are:

- The truth of suffering
- The truth of the cause of suffering
- The truth of the end of suffering
- The truth of the path that leads to the end of suffering.

To put it simply: suffering exists. It has a cause, it has an end, and it has a cause to bring about its end.

The notion of suffering is not intended to convey a negative worldview but a pragmatic perspective that deals with the world as it is and attempts to rectify it.

The Four Noble Truths offer a plan for dealing with the suffering humanity that faces—suffering of a physical kind or of a mental nature.

The First Truth identifies suffering. The Second Truth seeks to determine the cause of suffering.

The Third Truth, the truth of the end of suffering, has a dual meaning, suggesting either the end of suffering in this life on earth or in the spiritual life, through achieving nirvana.

The Fourth Truth charts the method for attaining the end of suffering, known to Buddhists as the Noble Eightfold Path.

The Noble Eightfold Path

The steps of the Noble Eightfold Path are:

- Right Understanding
- Right Thought
- Right Speech
- Right Action
- Right Livelihood
- Right Effort
- Right Mindfulness
- Right Concentration.

In addition, there are three areas into which the path is divided:

- Good moral conduct (Understanding, Thought, Speech)
- Meditation and mental development (Action, Livelihood, Effort)
- Wisdom or insight (Mindfulness and Concentration).

Karma

Karma is a word from the Sanskrit language that means "action." This can be to do something or say something, but it implies the cause and then the related effect of that action.

Karma is described as the relationship between cause and effect or actions and reactions. The theory of karma was around in India and the Hindu religion before the teachings of Buddha.

However, the forms of karma within Buddhism were formulated and explained by Buddha.

Buddhism teaches that karma results from our present doings and past actions. The core of karma is the understanding that a good action will have a good effect; however, a bad action will have a bad effect.

We are responsible for our actions, words, how we treat other living beings, and how we are perceived and treated by them.

We cause our own misery and happiness by our words and actions, and as such, we create our own heaven or hell.

In a practical sense, we see this occur every day of our lives and in the lives of people around us. How you treat other people and living creatures is how they will treat you. This is a form of practical karma that comes back to you quickly in your everyday life.

If you were angry at your boss or your job and quit, leaving on bad terms, you may not work at the company or get a good reference later in your life. You may find that boss moves to another company or knows people in other companies where you may be applying for jobs. Your past anger creates negative karma, which affects you in your future.

The Cycle of Rebirth

Karma plays out in the Buddhism cycle of rebirth. There are six separate realms into which any living being can be reborn. All realms are temporary, and it is not like heaven or hell in Christian religions. You move between the realms based on the karma you accumulate.

You don't have to believe in the reincarnation of the soul to understand rebirth. If you look at a photo of you as a baby, that was you. The same is true of a photo of you as a child, and when you look in the mirror now, that is still the same person. The body has changed, but the mind is still the same person. We are constantly changing states and being reborn.

Another easy-to-understand example is that, if we are overweight or unhealthy now, it results from our past actions of greed/overeating. This is a form of karma, which accumulated as we were changing states over the years. Our body has changed because of our past actions.

How we act, the words we speak, the people we are kind to, and the people we are mean to will affect our karma throughout our life as we constantly change states and are reborn.

The realms can be understood as a metaphor or state of mind, rather than a physical realm into which we are born. Which realm we are born into and live in is based on our actions and karma; however, all realms are temporary, and we are never in a realm for eternity.

Samsara

In literal terms, samsara means "wandering-on." It refers to the cycle of birth and rebirth that all living creatures go through based on karma.

Samsara ends if a person attains enlightenment and reaches nirvana.

Nirvana

Nirvana is the goal the Buddha reached during enlightenment, and he passed through nirvana after his death.

Nirvana refers to unbinding or extinguishing and implies that you receive freedom from whatever binds you.

Once nirvana and spiritual enlightenment have been reached, all debts or accumulated karma are extinguished, and you obtain a transcendent state, free from suffering and our worldly cycle of birth and rebirth.

3

THE FOUR NOBLE TRUTHS

"People have a hard time letting go of their suffering. Out of fear of the unknown, they prefer suffering that is familiar."
– Thich Nhat Hanh

THE FOUR NOBLE Truths come from the first teachings of Buddha after he obtained enlightenment. They teach about suffering and the end of suffering and are key lessons in the Buddhist religion.

The key points of the Four Noble Truths are:

1. The truth of suffering
2. The causes of suffering
3. The end of suffering
4. The path to obtain freedom from suffering.

In Buddhism, desire and ignorance lie at the root of suffering.

By desire, Buddhists refer to craving pleasure, material goods, and immortality, which are wants that can never be satisfied. Desiring them can only bring suffering.

Ignorance, in comparison, relates to not seeing the world as it is. Without the capacity for mental concentration and insight, Buddhism explains, one's mind is left undeveloped, unable to grasp the true nature of things. Vices, such as greed, envy, hatred, and anger, derive from this ignorance.

The concept of pleasure is not denied but acknowledged as fleeting. The pursuit of pleasure can only continue what is ultimately an unquenchable thirst. The same logic belies an understanding of happiness. Only aging, sickness, and death are certain and unavoidable.

The First Noble Truth

Also called the dukkha, this first Noble Truth translates to the definition of suffering. While the actual meaning of dukkha may be difficult to describe, the essence is very much the same. Every time you experience stress, discomfort, disease, tension, sadness, anger—basically any feeling or event that causes a person to feel pain and a lack of regret over something—it is part of the dukkha. Nobody is free from the dukkha; traces of suffering are found the moment you become aware of your existence.

How you understand the knowledge of your suffering makes a lot of difference, though. You must learn to investigate the origin of suffering and why you cannot extricate suffering from your life. Through learning, you harness the meaning of suffering and see the many cosmic patterns it weaves throughout your life.

For instance, say you have become so invested in becoming the perfect student that you study for hours each day. You participate in almost all discussions and thrust yourself into the hustle and bustle of activity. It may seem satisfying at first, especially when you notice people recognize your efforts.

But with a slight rejection or feeling of dissatisfaction, you might become hostile. You might also feel hopeless or betrayed. Once you start feeling negative, you feel the full blast of the dukkha. Often, the result is to separate yourself from other people, or from your former ideology, lest you suffer more.

The Second Noble Truth

The dukkha then leads you to the second Noble Truth—the cause of the suffering. This means dukkha doesn't happen without any triggers; pain does not come from thin air. There is a root to every feeling you experience. It is important that you understand how karmic forces and energy are in play now.

You might be wondering why you hate people so much that you have cut ties with the people you used to care about. This could have been caused by karma. The reason may not be obvious to you now, but through patterns and similar behaviors and responses, you can easily check for clues.

According to the teachings of Buddha, there are three

causes of suffering. These three "poisons," as they are called, bring aversion, craving, and confusion. They clutter the mind and strongly influence how you think, feel, and act.

For example, being clingy towards other people is an example of suffering. You become uneasy whenever you are alone or whenever your security is threatened. This feeling could have resulted from a breakup or a major separation, either between you and your partner or between your parents. Regardless of the truth behind this dukkha, you could crave attention and stability in a relationship.

Another example of the second Noble Truth is an aversion to commitment. You might find that forging ties with other people and staying committed and morally responsible for them has given you more stress than peace of mind. When this suffering is not healed, you might always feel an aversion towards anything that represents ties—marriage, romantic relationships, promises, and even job contracts.

The Third Noble Truth

In this stage, you are highly aware of where your dukkha is coming from, and it's time to put an end to it. You have diagnosed the problem. If you don't treat it, then the wound will just fester and eat you up, and you will be unable to heal.

In the teachings of Buddha, it is essential that you practice letting go of your dukkha. At some point, you must be mature and understand yourself more. It's not enough that you know the cause of your suffering.

This is the call to uproot the problem and gradually adjust and walk towards the path to healing. While the journey won't be smooth sailing, it's worth the try. Look at your suffering as a sinking ship; sometimes, the best move is simply to abandon it because it's not making you any better.

The Fourth Noble Truth

This final truth is the "actual prescription" to put an end to your dukkha. This is the total end of all your suffering. However, this isn't something you do temporarily. It requires great effort, commitment, and investment.

An example of committing to the fourth Noble Truth is living in accordance with the Eightfold Path and a spiritual life. You learn to meditate and deal with everyday suffering as if it's a part of the universe.

Anything negative happening to you isn't perceived as negative, but as part of the cosmos that contributes to your strength. With the final Noble Truth, you accept yourself and your flaws, and you feel no pain for being different, for being yourself, or for being human.

The Noble Truths and the Eightfold Path

Learning about these teachings not only makes you a better person but also gives more essence to your life. These things tell you that it's not about you, but about how you see yourself in this world—you have an important role to play.

You can achieve happiness—nirvana—only if you have

changed your ways and have attained all it takes to deserve this peace.

All these Noble Truths lead to yet another set of Buddha's teachings: the Eightfold Path. This is the ultimate path to end all suffering. This is where you will learn how best to frame your mind, thoughts, words, actions, and habits.

4

THE EIGHTFOLD PATH

"I teach one thing: suffering and its end." – **The Buddha**

ONE OF THE primary teachings of Buddhism calls for an end to suffering. Based on the Four Noble Truths, people can end suffering by letting go of worldly desires.

The Eightfold Path is a guide that aims to help one achieve this goal. It is a blueprint of how to live in accordance with the philosophy of Buddhism.

The elements of the Eightfold Path are:

1. Right Understanding

This means you should see the world for what it is. By developing a clearer understanding of your surroundings, you can gain a deeper understanding of your own self. This involves being attuned to your actions—from the reasons behind them to the way that they take effect.

This also involves a conscious effort to relinquish any thoughts and desires related to the concept of permanence and accept that all things change. By letting go of the desire for permanence, you can let go of the different illusions that cause you to be unhappy.

2. Right Thought

With the Buddhist mantra focused on not creating more suffering within yourself and in the world, you should actively seek to become more mindful of your intentions when dealing with others or deciding how to act. You should have full control over your actions.

Ask yourself whether your intentions are only for your own benefit or for the good of all. Remember that actions that arise from greed, resentment, or anger cause more harm than good. As they say, think before you speak or act. This will take time to master, so you must give yourself time for sufficient practice.

3. Right Speech

There's no truth to the saying, "It's only words," for words are never just words. When you utter something bad, it can easily have a negative impact on the person who hears it—sometimes, even without you realizing it. A single word can do enough damage to break one's spirit. This is why you should think before speaking.

Aside from saying something that may offend or hurt another person, you should also avoid lying to people.

Whenever you speak, make it a point to utter words that will be meaningful to others, including yourself. Make sure your statements have something positive to contribute to the lives of those with whom you are conversing.

4. Right Action

When your intentions are good, the effort you put into your actions will be skillful, and the outcome will be better than usual. This is why you should pay attention to your thoughts and focus on the positive aspects of things. As your thoughts heavily influence your actions, having the right intention will lead you to make the right actions.

Do not take this as someone ordering you to act a certain way. Take the time to meditate, learn, and develop a better ethical persona—with better judgment. Focus on helping others before yourself and take action if it benefits all. Do not forget that, if everyone benefits from your actions, you do too, and you gain something extra: the reward of fulfillment and joy.

5. Right Livelihood

It is not enough for you to have the right mindset and words or take the right actions. Work towards achieving a complete shift of lifestyle. Living honestly will enable you to help more people instead of being a source of harm. It is important for you to make an effort not to live to get rich.

For example, try not to engage in illegal trade, weapons dealing, prostitution, slavery, or endeavors that lead to violating other's rights. Be of service to others and treat your colleagues with dignity and respect.

6. Right Effort

It can be very difficult for you to achieve your goals if the right effort is not invested in your actions. This will hinder you from doing good where good can be done. Effort is an important element in the Eightfold Path of Buddhism. As a way to ease suffering in the world, you must have the right motivation or drive to want to do something meaningful.

If you have this driving force behind you, temptations from greed, jealousy, and whatnot will not have such a strong effect on you. You will be more in control of your speech and actions.

7. Right Mindfulness

When you are mindful, you can look at yourself from a different perspective. Mindfulness enables you to keep an open mind, focus on the present, and stay away from judgment. You should learn how to pay attention but understand that the art of mindfulness goes beyond alertness to what's going on around you.

It is choosing to be in control, rather than falling victim to distractions. Practicing being mindful keeps you grounded in the present and focused on what you must do to make a difference in this world. The best way to foster mindfulness is by meditating.

8. Right Concentration

One of the most important things in Buddhism is regular meditation, and this is at the center of the path to right concentration. Try your best to focus your mind on objects one at a time. Mindfulness calls for an openness to the world but also calls for the ability to focus on one thing amidst possible distractions from the world.

By meditating, you can condition your mind to control your reaction to distractions. This will help you sharpen your mind, making you more observant, alert, and in control of the things happening within your environment.

If you want to change your life, review the components of the Eightfold Path every now and then. Focus on areas where you feel you might be falling short. Practice those which you are closer to perfecting.

Always remember that these are simply guidelines to help make you a better person. They are not strict rules carved out in stone. Remember that Buddhism gives value to the establishment of faith in the human mind. You know what is right from wrong, so you just have to condition yourself to see things clearly to gain a better and more meaningful existence.

5

THE FIVE PRECEPTS

"One is not called noble who harms living beings.
Only by not harming living beings one is called noble."
— The Buddha

The Five Precepts

THE FIVE PRECEPTS are the key ethical guidelines of Buddhism; they are guidelines of how to live your life and how to act towards others. Unlike the Ten Commandments, there is no punishment from a god for breaking these rules. While a god won't punish you, breaking these rules can be seen as creating bad karma that will accumulate.

This need not be interpreted as purely cosmic karma. This is practical and logical. If you lie, cheat, or steal, you will eventually get caught; people will treat you as liar, cheater, or thief. It will also weigh heavily on your conscience, hiding these lies and betrayals and constantly trying to keep from being caught, so even if you get away with it in the short-term, it will have long-term consequences.

If you break these rules, you should reflect on them and find ways to rectify the situation and avoid doing this in the future, so over time, you constantly become better at living by these rules. These rules are for peace of mind and happiness for you and those around you.

As you learn to live in accordance with the five precepts, you will live your life with compassion in a harmonious manner.

1. Avoid harming living beings.

This teaching refers to all living beings—humans, animals, and any living creatures. This teaching implies you should act in a nonviolent way in all areas of your life.

Many Buddhists are vegetarian, and this rule can also be interpreted as not contributing to the death of anything living by destroying the natural world around us.

Buddhists teach us to show love and kindness towards all creatures, and at the essence of this teaching is this quote from the Dalai Lama:

> *"Our prime purpose in this life is to help others. And if you can't help them, at least don't hurt them."* – ***The Dalai Lama***

2. Avoid taking what is not given.

Don't steal from others, don't take more than is fair, and don't try to achieve wealth, power, fame, or success at the expense of other people.

Not stealing is easy to do, but there are other times you might not think about it, where you take what isn't fair.

Perhaps you received more than the correct change from a shop and you think that, because they gave you the wrong change, you are entitled to it; however, this is also a form of stealing and not fair to the other people as someone else may get blamed and be in trouble for stealing due to a mistake in calculating change.

3. Avoid harmful sexual activity.

Buddhism doesn't say you shouldn't have sex or enjoy sex. Buddhism teaches us to enjoy sex and be accepting of our sexuality and of other's sexuality.

This teaching means you should not engage in sexual activity that harms others or yourself. You should not commit sexual crimes; pressure people into sex if they are not comfortable; be pressured into sex if you are not comfortable; watch pornography; engage the services of prostitutes where others are harmed or pressured into sexual acts they are not comfortable with; or commit adultery.

Buddhism doesn't discourage you from enjoying sex or your sexuality, so long as it is healthy, consensual, and enjoyable for you and the other person.

4. Avoid saying what is not true.

We should avoid lying to others, including when we speak to others or write anything in print, online, or write text messages to other people.

We should not tell lies about other people or ourselves. We should not spread rumors or tell lies about anyone.

We should also not lie to ourselves. If you are in an abusive or unhealthy relationship and tell yourself that it will get better or it's not that bad, we know deep down we are lying to ourselves.

Lying to ourselves can also include smaller things, including times when we are trying to quit smoking or drinking and say we have no problem, we can quit whenever we want, but we have no evidence of being able to quit. So, this is a lie we tell. The same can be said if we want to start a positive gym habit and decide we won't go today but tell ourselves we will go tomorrow. This is how we lie to ourselves to feel better, but over time, this causes us harm.

It can be hard, at first, to be truthful with others and ourselves, but the initial hardship of confronting difficult truths is much better than small lies that get worse over time until we wish we could go back and just tell the truth at the start.

5. Avoid clouding your mind with alcohol or drugs.

Buddhism teaches we shouldn't get addicted to drugs, alcohol, or anything that can take control of our life, harm our body, mind, and cause us to hurt others.

When people become addicted to drugs and alcohol, they are unaware of the damage it does to them, along with the pain and suffering it causes to family and friends.

Your mind is precious, and you should take care of your health, including your mind and body. Any substances that harm your mind or body will affect your decisions, emotions, and how you live your life and treat others.

"When we feel love and kindness toward others, it not only makes others feel loved and cared for, but it helps us also to develop inner happiness and peace."

– The Dalai Lama

6

THE MIDDLE WAY

"On life's journey, faith is nourishment; virtuous deeds are a shelter; wisdom is the light by day; and right mindfulness is the protection by night. If a man lives a pure life, nothing can destroy him." – **The Buddha**

DURING THE TIME of the Buddha, holy men believed worldly desires prevented spiritual enlightenment and must be forsaken to live a spiritual life. The Buddha tried to find enlightenment through deprivation of worldly goods, including food.

He practiced extreme fasting, eating little food for six years. Collapsing in a river due to hunger and almost drowning was a turning point from a life of depriving himself of food to obtaining enlightenment.

The Buddha realized neither excess nor deprivation would lead to a spiritual life.

It was at this time that he saw a musician's lute (similar

guitar). He saw that if the string was too loose, then there would be no sound, but if the string was too tight, then it would break if played.

The key to playing the instrument was for the string to be neither too tight nor too loose. Either extreme would cause problems, and the only way was in the middle.

This is the key teaching of the Middle Way; it is moderation and not a path of excess or deprivation, moving away from the extremes on both sides and moving towards the middle.

The Middle Way refers to the enlightened view of life held by the Buddha and the attitudes or actions that will create contentment and happiness for yourself and others.

The teachings of Buddhism and the path of following the Middle Way involve the Eightfold Path, rejecting the extremes.

Rejection of the Extremes

The Buddha was fortunate to be born into a royal family as a prince, exposing him to a life of luxury. However, after choosing to live a spiritual life, he gave up the luxuries for a life of poverty.

It is the rejection of these extremes, and all extremes in life, that leads to the Middle Way.

When you eat food, eat enough to sustain you and be healthy; do not deprive yourself of food, but do not eat to excess.

This can apply to all areas of your life. Exercise is important to sustain your health. If you deprive yourself of physical activity, you will get sick and be unwell; however, if you push yourself to extremes, you can injure yourself and will become unwell.

It is the Middle Way of moderation with every area of your life that leads to living a healthy and fulfilled life.

"Master your senses,

What you taste and smell,

What you see, what you hear.

In all things be a master.

Of what you do and say and think.

Be free."

– The Buddha

7

MINDFULNESS

"In today's rush, we all think too much—seek too much—want too much—and forget about the joy of just being."
 — **Eckhart Tolle**

THE BASIS of mindfulness is the ability to be in the present moment and observe the sights, smells, sounds, and joy of not desiring to be anywhere else or having thoughts unrelated to where you are.

Practicing mindfulness is about directing the way you think about the world. Learning to live in the present moment and focusing your attention are the first steps towards mindfulness development.

Mindfulness encompasses witnessing the world around you without judging. When practicing mindfulness, it's important to observe and know what the mind and body are doing and come back to a state of awareness when your thoughts wander.

The opposite of mindfulness is mindlessness—becoming lost in what we are doing, distracted by random thoughts, and not having awareness of the present moment. We may become lost in thoughts of the future or the past or even lost in sights and noises that distract us.

When we become aware of what our mind is doing as an observer, we will not be distracted and lost in our thoughts and can be present and develop the right forms of concentration.

Steps for Mindful Practices

Use these steps to practice mindfulness:

Step #1: Be conscious of your focus and thoughts.

Make a conscious effort to concentrate on things and not let your mind wander. It's easy to get distracted and dwell on your feelings about the past or future. Learning to focus on the present moment is the first step to developing a mindfulness practice.

Step #2: Be aware of your actions.

Pay close attention to what you say and your actions, along with your motivations for these actions. Be aware of your urges for actions. If you are trying to write or read and you feel the urge to check Facebook, be aware of that urge. Realize it is distracting, and you are avoiding the task you are meant to be concentrating on, and bring the focus back to the task you are meant to be doing.

Step #3: Give your actions purpose (in your mind).

Purpose can be broad, depending on the task, but mainly involves the purpose of focusing your attention. As you accomplish your tasks, you must be present in your mind.

Taking your phone out of your pocket and checking social media can be a mindless habit—this is not mindfulness.

You may decide to take your phone out of your pocket to send an email, but then you get distracted and open Facebook; you then forget why you took your phone out and don't complete the task you intended.

Be aware of the tasks and actions you must do and do them with purpose, without mindless distractions.

If you are distracted, be aware of it, acknowledge it, and refocus your concentration back to the present.

Step #4: Stay in the present and stop living in the past.

If you dwell on the past, you can get caught up in a negative cycle of thinking that distracts you from the present moment.

You may have had situations where you can't sleep because you are constantly thinking about a situation that occurred earlier in the day.

You've probably experienced a negative conversation and interaction with another person and then thought, "I should have said that to them" and gone over the conversation again in your mind with all the things you wanted to say.

This negative thinking takes away your peace and enjoyment of the present moment.

It is difficult, but one method that can be helpful is, if you have a negative interaction with someone, think that they took a few minutes of your time with that negative encounter, but it's in the past, and you won't let them take any more of your time by dwelling on it.

You can't change the past; you must accept it, come to peace with it, and not dwell on it.

Step #5: Don't dwell on future events.

It is okay to plan a future, but use caution and don't let worries about a future ruin your present lifestyle.

Don't spend the present moment worrying and stressing about what might occur.

You may have experienced times when you couldn't sleep, you were stressed, and constantly worried about something in the future. However, when it happened, the things you worried about didn't occur, or they weren't as bad as you thought.

Afterwards, you may have thought to yourself, "I had no need to worry" or "That wasn't so bad." Often, the stress and worry about a situation that might occur turns out to be unfounded or worse than the actual event.

Step #6: Don't be a clock-watcher.

"Life is what happens to you when you're busy making other plans."
— Allen Saunders

As mentioned in step seven, often, we don't enjoy the present moment because we are too caught up in worrying about the future.

The same is true about planning the future, even if we look forward to it.

For example, if you have booked a holiday that is a month away, you may spend that month counting down the days until that holiday, spending your moments thinking about the holiday and how you wish you were already there, instead of where you are now.

However, if we put high expectations on our holiday, we may not enjoy it as much, as we have spent so much time planning an idea of how amazing it will be before it happens.

By constantly looking forward to relaxing in the future, instead of now, we may also miss the time to relax in the park or time with friends that would provide as much enjoyment or relaxation as the holiday we have imagined.

We can do this on a smaller basis, such as waiting for the train. We think it's just time waiting, so we do mindless activities like check social media or play a video game to fill the time.

When we have a task we don't enjoy at work or are in a

meeting for an hour, we may count down the time, constantly checking the clock to see when it will end.

We may not enjoy the task we are doing because it is difficult; however, if we think of that difficulty as learning and expanding our skill set, then we can approach it differently, and we may enjoy it.

We spend a lot of our life worrying about the future or longing for the future, instead of being focused on the moment. By being focused on the present moment, instead of longing for the future, we can experience a fuller life, instead of letting it slip by while we make other plans.

Step #7: Take a break and have some alone time.

We are constantly around people all day. Even when we get home and are by ourselves, we turn on the TV or watch videos online with people.

Taking time out of the day to relax by yourself, disconnect from technology, and just be with yourself can be very calming and relaxing.

You can go on a walk, practice breathing exercises, or meditate. Doing this during the day, even for a few moments, can help reduce stress and revitalize you for the rest of the day.

Step #8: Don't pass judgment, just pay attention.

Part of being mindful is noticing what goes on around you without placing judgment on it.

Our mind is automatically judging things as good or

bad. We automatically judge people based on the job they do or our limited interaction with them.

We may see a homeless person on the street and automatically judge him and create a story in our head that it would be easy for that person to get a job if he wanted, but he is lazy or an alcoholic.

Then our judging thought pattern may continue, and we become angry at how hard we must work and how much we owe in taxes and how so many people in the world just expect to be given everything.

However, the reality is that we know nothing about the person, and we are making broad generalizations, judging, and attaching emotion to a story we created.

Have you ever gone to see a movie you were excited about and then been disappointed because the movie didn't live up to your expectations?

Have you ever been surprised at how much you enjoyed a movie because you expected it to be bad or had no expectations about it?

How many other situations has this occurred that you can think of because you judged something incorrectly before it occurred?

While it may be difficult to stop ourselves from automatically judging, we can be aware of when we are doing it and stop the thought pattern from continuing.

We can also notice when we are judging and creating stories in our mind. If we create a negative story in our head, we can create the opposite story to see the difference it makes to our view on the situation.

With both of those are stories, we can see the power

these stories we make up in our mind has over our emotions and experience by countering a negative story with a positive one.

Try to view everything around you in an objective manner. Notice when you are judging, then stop the judging thought pattern from continuing or affecting your view of the situation.

Step #9: Remember, mindfulness isn't always a happy thought pattern.

Practicing mindfulness means you are not dwelling on the past or future, regardless of whether the thought is positive or negative.

You may not be enjoying the present moment, so you focus on a future that may be more pleasant.

Mindfulness involves being present and aware of the present moment, observing your feelings and surroundings in the moment, even if they are not enjoyable.

Step #10: Observe your emotions.

It's commonly thought that Buddhist meditation and mindfulness practices involve getting rid of emotions.

However, you can't get rid of your emotions. The focus, therefore, is not on controlling your emotions, but on not letting yourself be controlled by your emotions.

For example, if you are feeling anger towards someone, you can observe that you are breathing faster; you are clenching your fists and grinding your teeth. You can observe yourself feeling angry and how it impacts your body.

You may not control the anger you feel, but you can stop it from controlling you and reacting to that emotion by yelling at the person or hurting him or her.

Step #11: Use compassion and kindness to others.

Understand that not everyone you encounter shares your outlook on life; your opinions are not facts. You can practice not judging other people or believing you are right and trying to convince other people they are wrong.

When you encounter people, don't judge them. Often people are experiencing difficult times you are not aware of that impact their moods and how they act.

You don't know everybody's story or situation, so you should practice nonjudgment, with compassion and empathy towards others.

Being mindful of your interactions with people is another step in nonjudgment and towards compassion and kindness.

There are numerous chances every day to practice kindness and compassion towards others. Even just giving someone a genuine smile can make a difference to that person's day.

Mindfulness Meditation

This form of meditation is to witness the 'wandering' thoughts as each drifts through your mind.

You only need to be aware of each of the thoughts involved: don't dwell on them; don't try to avoid bad thoughts; don't try to focus on good thoughts.

Don't become too immersed or judge your thoughts; just observe them and let them pass.

You may realize your feelings and thoughts have a certain pattern and see how you may judge whether an experience is good or bad.

Walking Meditation

"Walk as if you are kissing the earth with your feet."
— Thich Nhat Hanh

You may have been stressed or anxious about something in the past and felt you needed to go for a walk to calm yourself or clear your mind.

This is a form of mindfulness, known as walking meditation, that provides awareness of your mind and body and helps clear your thoughts and focus on the present moment.

Below are a few tips to provide you with a relaxing experience:

1. Search for a place where you can walk without obstacles or have to avoid people. A park is often a good place to walk.
2. Gather your thoughts for a few minutes, so you are consciously aware of the movements within your body. Observe how your clothes feel, your

feet feel on the ground, or how the leaves are gently rolling over each other on a fall day.

3. Walk slowly at a natural pace. Stay within your thoughts and move back to how your body feels.

4. Observe your surroundings—the sounds, sights, and smells—observing the wind blowing on you or the sun on your skin.

While it's tempting to listen to music or an audiobook when doing walking meditation, it's important to listen to the sounds around you and not be distracted from the present moment.

Mindfulness Eating and Drinking

"Drink your tea slowly and reverently, as if it is the axis on which the world earth revolves—slowly, evenly, without rushing toward the future; live the actual moment. Only this moment is life." – **Thich Nhat Hanh**

Often, when eating, we eat quickly while we are watching TV, on the computer, or distracted by other things. We eat fast and rarely observe much of the taste or texture.

With mindful eating, you take the time to notice the smell and appearance of the food. You take the time to eat slowly, observe the taste of the food, the texture; you chew slowly while focusing on eating and being present.

An experience that can provide heightened mindfulness when eating is to dine in a restaurant where you are in total darkness when eating. Your senses of taste and smell are enhanced, bringing heightened awareness to the taste and texture of the food.

Without going to a restaurant for this experience, you can also get a similar experience by closing your eyes when eating and focusing more intensely on the taste and texture of the food, with fewer distractions from the other senses and thoughts.

8

MEDITATION

"There are techniques of Buddhism, such as meditation, that anyone can adopt." – **The Dalai Lama**

MEDITATION IS an important part of Buddhism, and it is a common practice among almost all Buddhists.

While it is a part of Buddhism, meditation is not a religious practice, and as such, it has gained popularity among people of all religions.

In recent years, meditation has seen a large increase in popularity, helped in part by the number of celebrities and successful people who have adopted meditation.

Many practice meditation daily, claiming it has had immense benefits on their life and success. Despite how busy they are, many make time for daily meditation practice, often in the morning before starting their day.

We often find we have a constant stream of thoughts

rushing around our head. We may not sleep because we have a lot on our mind. During the day, we find our mind rushing from one thought to another.

Meditation helps to calm our mind, clear it of negative thoughts, gain clarity, achieve calm, and improve focus.

Meditation helps us achieve a peaceful state that allows a clearer focus on important thoughts and removes the noise and chaos from all the distracting or negative thoughts that constantly bombard our mind.

With regular practice, meditation has been shown to have significant positive physical changes on the brain, such as increasing gray matter in the brain in areas associated with learning, memory, and regulating emotions. There is also evidence that meditation helps boost the immune system, with other positive health benefits.

How to Meditate

Starting meditation can be difficult at first. It's hard to sit and try to clear your thoughts for long periods of time.

A story that examines how difficult this can be is about the man who goes to a meditation retreat.

On the first day, the monk tells the man that his aim is to focus on his breathing and clear his mind of thoughts for one minute. Once he can do that, he can do whatever he wants for the rest of the day.

The man sits down, takes a deep breath, and focuses on his breathing. After a few seconds, he thinks, "This is easy. I'll easily be able to do this."

He realizes he is thinking, so he starts again. After a few more seconds, he thinks, "I'm doing really well; when I finish this, I'll go read that book I brought."

This continues again and again: starting meditation, then thoughts popping into his head after a few seconds, and restarting the meditation practice.

The man spends the whole day unable to clear his thoughts for one minute.

You will most likely find the same thing happens to you when you start to develop a meditation practice. However, don't be discouraged. This is normal.

Meditation is like exercise. At first, your muscles may struggle with small weights, and you may feel you can never lift any larger weights. Over time, as you practice, you will find your muscles stretch and grow, becoming able to lift more weight.

The same is true with meditation. At first, you may be unable to clear your mind for a minute, but over time, you can increase the time you meditate, and you will find that your focus, concentration, and clarity will also grow.

Start small, make it a routine, and don't get discouraged if it seems difficult at first.

You will find meditation difficult at first, but by making a commitment to doing it daily, over time, you will see your ability to meditate develop and the positive effects increase.

Meditating around the same time, such as in the morning after waking up, and doing it for as little as five to ten minutes can make it easier to build into a routine.

Starting with guided meditation is important, so you understand how to build a correct technique of focusing on breathing. This book has many recommended resources to help you learn more about meditation and build a daily meditation practice.

While I recommend using the guided meditation in the resources chapter, there are methods you can use in everyday life to meditate on your own.

Simple Meditation for Beginners

This is the most common meditation practice. It involves sitting or being still in one place and focusing on the breath as you slowly breathe in and out to help calm and clear the mind.

- Close your eyes while you lie or sit comfortably. (Don't fall asleep.)
- Breathe naturally, making no effort to control your breathing patterns.
- This can be difficult when starting, so it's okay to take a big deep breath in and out and slowly adjust to natural breathing without controlling it.
- Focus on each breath and how your body moves as you inhale and exhale.
- Pay attention to the movement of each part of your body. Begin at your shoulders, then move down to the chest, then to the stomach and back up again, slowly noticing the movement of your body.

- Observe your breath without attempting to control its intensity or pace.
- If your thoughts wander, refocus your breathing and be aware of each movement. This is a key part of the practice. Don't worry if your mind wanders; just keep bringing your focus back to your breathing.
- Start with two to five minutes and increase the time as you become accustomed to the process.

Concentration Meditation

Concentration meditation can be helpful if you can't calm your thoughts during a regular sitting meditation.

It's often hard to stop our thoughts from wandering at the start when practicing meditation, so focusing on one word or object can help produce calm and clear the mind.

Focusing on one theme is the key to concentration meditation. A common practice is staring at the flame of a candle; however, this practice can be done with anything that produces serenity for you when you focus your attention on one thing.

If your mind begins to wander, don't chase your thoughts; just let them go. Refocus your awareness on your chosen object of attention. As you practice the method, your concentration will improve.

Meditation with a Mantra

A mantra is a phrase you repeat silently to yourself throughout the process of meditation.

If you are using a mantra, you need a focus placed on anything other than your thoughts. It is common to use the mantra phrase 'So Hum,' which is from Sanskrit and translates into English as 'I am.'

To meditate using a mantra, the method is like simple meditation or concentration meditation, but you use the mantra to help clear your thoughts and focus on that.

1. Get Comfortable

Find a discreet location away from any distractions. Sit comfortably (upright if possible) and begin the process.

2. Close Your Eyes

While your eyes are closed, take some deep breaths. Inhale slowly through your nose and exhale using your mouth. Breathe normally, at a relaxed pace, with your mouth closed.

3. Repeat the Mantra

Use your mind and be silent as you repeat your mantra using gentle, soft, and relaxed tones. The mantra should be an effortless rhythm. Think of it as if someone was whispering in your ear.

4. Cease the Mantra

After stopping the mantra, remain seated with your eyes closed and relax. You can use meditation timer apps for soothing sounds to replace the mantra if you choose.

Choose an amount of time for your meditation that is comfortable for you. As time passes—you can increase the time—even a few minutes will provide you with serenity and calm.

Daily Meditation Practice

The old saying "practice makes perfect" is very true. At first, it will be difficult, and you will feel that you're not doing it right. As you practice daily, you will notice you become calmer, the practice becomes easier, and you notice the benefits.

This has been touched upon several times in this book, but it's hard to start a new habit. Even though you know of the benefits of meditation, life often gets in the way, and we get caught up and busy and feel we don't have time or say that we'll do it later.

Start small and make it a routine. You don't have to meditate for an hour to do it correctly. Start with less than ten minutes a day, and it will be easier to sustain. You will notice the benefits, once it becomes a daily practice.

If you've ever stared into a campfire, sat on the beach watching the waves crash against the shore, or watched a sunset, then you have experienced a form of meditation.

You may have understood in those moments how it feels to be at peace with the world, your body, mind, and live in the present moment.

9

GRATITUDE

"We don't need more money; we don't need greater success or fame; we don't need the perfect body or even the perfect mate.

Right now, at this very moment, we have a mind, which is all the basic equipment we need to achieve complete happiness."

– The Dalai Lama

BUDDHISM TEACHES that gratitude is an essential part of being happy, feeling fulfilled, and being present in the moment.

When we are not grateful for what we have, we always want more. We live with our minds in the future, constantly longing for more money or different circumstances and believing, when we obtain that, we will then have happiness.

We live in a society that focuses on material wealth, where success is based on the money you have and the objects you own.

We may have a good cell phone, but then a newer model

phone comes out, and we're not happy with our current phone, as we want the latest version.

We may have a good job that pays well, but we want a promotion and a pay raise, thinking when we get that new job title and more money, we'll have more success and more happiness.

However, we may have thought the same before we got the job and salary.

The job we have may have even seemed like a dream job when we started our career. We may have thought, if we achieved a certain job title and income level, then we would have success and happiness.

We believe more wealth will lead to more happiness; however, as we obtain more income, we spend and want more, so enough income, success, and therefore happiness seems constantly out of reach with this perspective.

"When you are discontent, you always want more, more, more. Your desire can never be satisfied.

But when you practice contentment, you can say to yourself, 'Oh yes—I already have everything that I really need."

– The Dalai Lama

Even if we are not living in the future, our mind may be living in the past, thinking of a time when our situation made us happy, such as a relationship that has ended.

We may desire to be back, believing that was when we were happy, and we can never have that again, so we can never be that happy again.

There are countless studies that show dwelling on the

past and thinking about past circumstances can lead to depression. We are not living in the present reality when we do this. We withdraw from reality and the present moment and live in the past, being unhappy about our present circumstances.

The longer we continue to do this, the worse it gets; our negative emotions snowball, and our unhappiness about the present moment continues to grow.

To be happy, we must not live in the past or the future, but we must be grateful for what we have now.

This can be difficult in certain circumstances, such as a difficult life event, but we must accept that the past has gone, we cannot live in the future, and we have only the present moment.

We can start to be grateful for small things. There are many people in the world struggling to survive, many without food or clean water, who would love to be in your circumstances.

Gratitude can start with a small appreciation for what you have. This small appreciation will benefit your mood and mindset, and your happiness about your present moment will continue to grow.

*"Every day, think as you wake up: today, I am fortunate to have woken up. I am alive. I have a precious human life. I am not going to waste it." – **The Dalai Lama***

Everyone has the opportunity and ability to develop gratitude simply by focusing on good parts of your life and what you already have.

A simple practice to start is, every day, write down things you are grateful for. This could just be one thing, and it doesn't even have to seem significant to you. It could be something you take for granted, like you are grateful that you have a shelter and a bed to sleep in.

The simplest method to improve the satisfaction levels in your life is through gratitude. Look around where you are now and think about what you have in your life. You can get a pen and paper and write down one thing in your life now that you are grateful for.

Now think about what you wrote down and feel gratitude for just that for a moment. Don't think about the future or dwell on the past; just think about what you have written and feel grateful for that.

You can achieve more happiness by writing down one thing every day, either in the morning or at night, so you start the day on a positive note or go to sleep with a positive thought in your mind. This simple daily practice has been shown to achieve higher levels of happiness with little effort.

"Let's rise and be thankful, for if we didn't learn a lot today, at least we may have learned a little.

And if we didn't learn even a little, at least we didn't get sick.

And if we did get sick, at least we didn't die.

So let us all be thankful."

– Buddhist monk, quote by Leo Buscaglia

10

BUDDHISM IN EVERYDAY LIFE

"Appreciate how rare and full of potential your situation is in this world, then take joy in it, and use it to your best advantage."
— Dalai Lama

TO PRACTICE Buddhism and Buddhist practices in everyday life, you don't have to change your life or routines.

You can start with simple practices, such as gratitude, mindfulness, meditation, affirmations, or positive thinking.

When starting new practices, it is best not to overwhelm yourself; otherwise, they won't stick. Don't try to meditate for an hour each day, along with all the other practices.

Start with small practices and build from there until it becomes a habit and routine.

As mentioned in the previous chapter on gratitude, you can start by writing down just one thing you are grateful for.

It's beneficial to incorporate practices at the same time every day to build a habit.

A practice at the start of the day can set a positive tone that stays with you throughout the day.

A practice at the end of the day can calm your mind and thoughts, helping you achieve positive sleep and rest, which then flows into the next day.

The next part of this chapter will outline some benefits of a few practical Buddhist practices that are very applicable to everyday life and how to incorporate them into your life.

There are many practices but covered here are only a few practical exercises you can easily start to help you become calmer, less stressed, more aware of your words and actions and how you treat other people.

Again, remember, you don't have to change your life significantly. Start small and keep up a small practice until it becomes a daily habit.

The positive effects of just one practice, when done daily, will grow and have a beneficial effect on other aspects of your life.

"Great suffering leads to compassion,

Great compassion makes a peaceful heart,

A peaceful heart makes a peaceful person,

A peaceful person makes a peaceful family,

A peaceful family makes a peaceful community,

A peaceful community makes a peaceful nation,

A peaceful nation makes a peaceful world."

– Maha Ghosananda, Buddhist Monk

Mindfulness

Mindfulness is a broad term but can be understood to be

a mental state achieved by focusing on awareness of the present moment in a calm state of acceptance of feelings, thoughts, and sensations of the body.

To be mindful, you are aware and paying attention, with your focus present in the moment or situation, not letting your mind wander with unrelated thoughts.

We are often caught up in our thoughts, dwelling on things that have happened or worrying about the future, and we are not enjoying or focused on the present moment.

Mindfulness helps bring us back to the present moment to concentrate on what is going on around us and to enjoy our surroundings.

Benefits of Mindfulness

- Helps clear your mind and calm your thoughts
- Allows you to manage difficult emotions
- Allows you to be more focused
- Helps you be more aware of your words and actions
- Improves how you interact with people
- Increases self-insight and understanding of yourself
- Reduces stress and achieves calmness
- Reduce fears and improves your ability to manage emotions
- Leads to greater relationship satisfaction
- Clarifies thoughts so they're less confused and erratic

- Allows you to focus on what is important, rather than what seems urgent all the time
- Helps you be better able to think before reacting to events
- Enhances brain function
- Reduces psychological stress
- Increases information processing
- Decreases distraction and reduces thoughts not connected to the job at hand
- Decreases task switching and trying to get too much done at once

How to be Mindful in Everyday Life

As mentioned, when starting any habit or practice, it's important not to do too much at once. It's important to build a small routine that is sustainable.

With mindfulness, it is useful in reducing stress and ensuring you have focused attention and awareness. This need not be all the time, but you can take time at the start of the day when you wake up to breathe and focus on your breath. Doing this for even one to two minutes can start your day with calm.

During the day, we are bombarded with phone calls, emails, instant messages, and notifications. A way to be mindful is when focused on a task, to focus solely on that task without distractions.

When reading this book, notice the notifications that pop up and think about whether you need to see those all the time. You can turn some off, so you are not so distracted all the time.

When on your phone, notice your mind thinking about switching to another app or the desire to go to a website, then take a deep breath, let that thought pass, and continue focusing on reading this book.

Multitasking, task switching, and flipping between work, without focusing or finishing, causes a great deal of stress and a lack of productivity.

Often, we get to work feeling stressed and feeling we have a lot to do. We feel busy all day, believing we are working hard, yet at the end of the day, we didn't do the important things that we needed to do. We wonder how we could be working so hard and be so stressed, yet not get anything important done.

You can avoid this by writing down an important task you want to complete at the start of the day and scheduling in time to complete it. Treat this task like a meeting, turning off emails, notifications, and phone calls, and focusing only on that task.

Emails can wait for a few hours before you reply. Most of the time, you can batch your emails and reply to many all at once, instead of constantly being notified of them.

This practice can be incorporated into many areas of your life. If you are watching television while trying to study, turn off the TV and focus on your studies.

You may trick yourself into feeling you study better when there is a TV on in the background; however, this is rarely the case. If your focus is split between the TV and your study, it will often result in completing tasks slower, at a lower quality, while putting more stress on the mind.

Practice giving the task you are working on your full focus, and you will notice the difference.

If you are getting angry or stressed about something, notice that stress and anger, take a deep breath, and focus on your breathing and be aware of your emotions and surroundings.

Another easy way to be mindful is simply to take a walk in a park or just around the street, without headphones or notifications, and just take in the sights and sounds around you.

Practicing mindfulness can include a variety of practices that need not be complicated or take a long time. Start small, try to be more present, less distracted, and this will help you feel less stressed, calmer, and more mindful in everyday life.

Meditation

As mentioned, many famous and successful people meditate daily, as they strongly believe that even a short meditation session has huge positive benefits.

Some benefits of meditation found when studying people that meditate daily are outlined below.

Benefits of Meditation

- Improves concentration

- Increases ability to focus for longer periods of time
- Improves memory
- Reduces stress
- Decreases anxiety
- Increases happiness levels
- Lowers rates of depression
- Affords more clarity on important tasks
- Lessens anger and improves ability to control mood
- Improves sleep and ability to get to sleep easier
- Improves cognitive skills, creative thinking, and decision-making
- Improves health and immune system including lower blood pressure, blood circulation, heart rate, and respiratory rate

How to Build a Meditation Practice

When starting a meditation practice, it's important to start small and make it a routine. This is the same for any daily habit or practice you wish to start.

At the start, it may seem difficult to meditate, or you may feel you are not doing it correctly or can't find the time. However, just start by making a commitment to a daily practice around the same time for as little as five to ten minutes.

When starting, I would recommend not trying to do more than ten minutes at a time.

You can start with less than five minutes; however, it

helps at the start to use guided meditation lessons or apps to help you build the practice and method correctly. Apps such as Headspace take around ten minutes for their daily guided practice.

In chapter 12, there is a wide range of resources, such as apps and websites, to help learn more about meditation and build a daily meditation practice.

Gratitude

Gratitude can be practiced in many ways. You can be grateful for what you have; you can be grateful for other people; you can also show gratitude towards others or develop a sense of gratitude about the world and your everyday life.

Benefits of Gratitude

Gratitude has many benefits that may not seem obvious at first. It's hard to see how being grateful will affect your body like exercise, but studies show people that are consistently grateful see positive effects in both their physical and mental health.

Some reasons there are so many benefits to gratitude can be attributed to the fact that, when you are grateful, your mind changes the way you perceive the world around you. You are happier with what you have. You also change the way you interact with people and appreciate them more, and they sense this, which reflects how they treat you.

Increases happiness – Many people live in a mindset

of never having enough, being unhappy with what they have, and always wanting more. When you are grateful for what you have, instead of thinking about what you don't have, then your happiness levels dramatically increase. This is a key factor as to why gratitude has such positive effects.

Reduces negative emotions – Along with an increase in happiness, gratitude reduces negative emotions, such as depression, envy, anger, regret, and feeling inadequate. Gratitude is not just being thankful that you have enough in your life, but knowing that you, as a person, are enough, which makes you happier about yourself and reduces negative emotions.

Improves sleep – If you've found yourself unable to sleep because of negative thoughts in your head, dwelling on the past, or worrying about the future, then you may find practicing gratitude before sleep can help you sleep easier.

To practice gratitude at night, you can write down things you are grateful for or focus on grateful thoughts. This will change the focus of your mind and thoughts to more peaceful and relaxed thoughts, which will help you get to sleep faster and sleep better during the night.

Strengthens positive emotions – When your thoughts change from thoughts of not having enough to thoughts of gratitude for what you have, you will find your general emotions and feelings about many areas of your life and situations will be more positive.

Stress will be reduced, and when you encounter difficult times or obstacles, you will feel more optimistic and overcome these challenges easier.

Improves personality – When you are more grateful

for what you have and your friends and family, you will find you appreciate the things you have and the people in your life more.

This will lead to changes in how you treat people, how you deal with situations, and how other people perceive you when they are around you.

Improves self-esteem – When you are grateful for what you have, instead of constantly comparing yourself to others and feeling inadequate, you gain self-esteem about what you have.

Being jealous of someone else having a newer car, newer phone, higher-paying job, or bigger home, etc., will make you unhappy, begrudge that person, and make you feel inadequate. When you stop this behavior and mindset, you will be grateful for what you have, and then you will gain self-esteem.

Improves relationships – When you show gratitude towards other people, they will feel appreciated by you. They will want to be around you and will be happy to help you. Being grateful for other people and expressing this gratitude towards them will improve your relationships, friendships, and encounters with people you meet.

How to Start a Practice of Gratitude

Starting a practice of gratitude can be as simple as writing down one thing you are grateful for in the morning or before you go to bed. Practicing gratitude at the start of the day is beneficial, as this can set the mindset for the rest of the day and influence a grateful and positive mindset for the rest of the day.

Practicing gratitude at the end of the day will help settle you, help you avoid negative thoughts, and focus you on things you are grateful for. This will help you sleep easier and feel more rested when you wake the next day.

You can practice gratitude throughout the day by thinking about the things you are grateful for when they occur. Even having food, a job, and shelter are things to be grateful for.

Expressing gratitude for other people is another way to practice gratitude. When you are at work and someone helps you with something, express gratitude and thank them. Let them know you appreciate the time and effort it took them.

You can express gratitude towards everyone you encounter throughout the day, e.g., at a restaurant, you can let the person that served you know you appreciate his service and thank him. Even leaving a 'gratuity' (tip) is a form of showing gratitude.

We should treat people how we would like to be treated, and expressing gratitude to others is an important aspect of developing a mindset of gratitude.

Buddhist Teaching and Practices in Everyday Life

*"As the bee takes the essence of a flower and flies away without destroying its beauty and perfume, so the sage wanders in life." – **The Buddha***

While mindfulness, meditation, and gratitude are practiced by many Buddhists and often go hand in hand with Buddhism, they are also practiced by people with no exposure to Buddhist teachings.

There are many Buddhist teachings directly from the Buddha that can also be incorporated into everyday life, without a dramatic change to how you live.

We covered the five precepts and the Noble Eightfold Path earlier in the book. These teachings are core Buddhist teachings, and it's important to know of these and practice them.

1. Avoid harming living beings.
2. Avoid taking what is not given.
3. Avoid harmful sexual activity.
4. Avoid saying what is not true.
5. Avoid clouding your mind with alcohol or drugs.

The Middle Way teaches moderation with all things and not doing anything to excess.

While you shouldn't cloud your mind with alcohol, a glass of wine with dinner is okay; however, getting drunk and drinking to where it affects our lives should be avoided.

If you often get drunk on a weekend or drink too much occasionally, you could try limiting yourself to one drink, or you could try a challenge of not drinking any alcohol for thirty days and see the effect on your body, mind, health, and relationships.

The five precepts are also connected to the Eightfold Path; however, as this is an introduction, these simple practices and teachings should be enough to incorporate Buddhism into your life and see positive effects without needing to make large changes to how you live your life.

"Our prime purpose in this life is to help others. And if you can't help them, at least don't hurt them." – **The Dalai Lama**

11

BUDDHIST QUOTES

Quotes from the Buddha:

"All that we are is the result of our thoughts. If you speak or act with an evil thought, pain follows you. If you speak or act with a pure thought, happiness follows you. The result of your thoughts is like a shadow that never leaves you."

"Holding onto anger is like holding onto a hot coal waiting to throw it at someone else; in the end, you are the one who gets burned."

"All experiences are preceded by mind, having mind as their master, created by mind."

"Just as a mother would protect her only child with her life, even so let one cultivate a boundless love towards all beings."

"Radiate boundless love towards the entire world …"

"Speak only endearing speech, speech that is welcomed. Speech, when it brings no evil to others, is a pleasant thing."

"Do today what must be done, for who knows about tomorrow, perhaps death comes."

"If you propose to speak, always ask yourself, is it true? Is it necessary? Is it kind?"

"Give, even if you only have a little."

"Worrying doesn't take away tomorrow's troubles; it takes away today's peace."

"Meditate … do not delay, lest you later regret it."

"One is not called noble who harms living beings. By not harming living beings, one is called noble."

"A disciplined mind brings happiness."

"Conquer anger with non-anger. Conquer badness with goodness. Conquer meanness with generosity. Conquer dishonesty with truth."

"When you look after yourself, you look after others. When you look after others, you look after yourself."

"All living beings tremble at violence, and all fear death. Always put yourself in the place of another; you should not kill or cause another to kill."

"Understand that you, along with all others, will die; once you realize this, you will settle your quarrels."

"Do not find fault with others; do not see the omissions and commissions of others. But instead see your own acts, both done and undone."

"All wrongdoing arises because of mind. If mind is transformed, can wrongdoing remain?"

Quotes from the Dalai Lama:

"Be kind whenever possible and remember, it is always possible."

"Our prime purpose in this life is to help others. And if you can't help them, at least don't hurt them."

"Happiness is not something ready-made. It comes from your own actions."

"People take different roads seeking fulfillment and

happiness. Just because they're not on your road doesn't mean they've gotten lost."

"My religion is very simple. My religion is kindness."

"When we meet real tragedy in life, we can react in two ways—either by losing hope and falling into self-destructive habits or by using the challenge to find our inner strength. Thanks to the teachings of Buddha, I have been able to take this second way."

"Remember that sometimes, not getting what you want is a wonderful stroke of luck."

"Everything you do has some effect, some impact."

"We can never obtain peace in the outer world until we make peace with ourselves."

"Only the development of compassion and understanding for others can bring us the tranquility and happiness we all seek."

"Every day, think as you wake up, 'Today, I am fortunate to have woken up. I am alive. I have a precious human life. I am not going to waste it.'"

"If a problem is fixable, if a situation is such that you can do something about it, then there is no need to worry. If it's not fixable, then there is no help in worrying. There is no benefit in worrying whatsoever."

"Love and compassion are necessities, not luxuries. Without them, humanity cannot survive."

"There are only two days in the year that nothing can be done. One is called yesterday and the other is called tomorrow, so today is the right day to love, believe, do, and mostly, live."

Quotes from Thich Nhat Hanh:

"To be beautiful, means to be yourself. You don't need to be accepted by others. You need to accept yourself."

"When another person makes you suffer, it is because he suffers deeply within himself, and his suffering is spilling over. He does not need punishment; he needs help. That's the message he is sending."

"Sometimes your joy is the source of your smile, but sometimes your smile can be the source of your joy."

"Letting go gives us freedom, and freedom is the only condition for happiness. If, in our heart, we still cling to anything—anger, anxiety, or possessions—we cannot be free."

"Root out the violence in your life, and learn to live compassionately and mindfully. Seek peace. When you have peace within, real peace with others is possible."

"When you smile, you make life more beautiful."

"When you love someone, the best thing you can offer is your presence. How can you love if you are not there? If you love someone but rarely make yourself available to him or her, that is not true love."

"People sacrifice the present for the future. But life is available only in the present. That is why we should walk in such a way that every step can bring us to the here and the now."

"When you learn about the teaching and the practice of another tradition, you always have a chance to understand your own teaching and practice."

"You know that your happiness and suffering depend on the happiness and suffering of others. That insight helps you not to do wrong things that will bring suffering to yourself and to other people."

"People have a hard time letting go of their suffering. Out of a fear of the unknown, they prefer suffering that is familiar."

"People suffer because they are caught in their views. As

soon as we release those views, we are free and we don't suffer anymore."

"Waking up this morning, I smile. Twenty-four brand-new hours are before me. I vow to live fully in each moment and to look at all beings with eyes of compassion."

"I promise myself that I will enjoy every minute of the day that is given me to live."

12

MEDITATION APPS AND RESOURCES

"Do not dwell in the past, do not dream of the future, concentrate the mind on the present moment." – **The Buddha**

FOR THOUSANDS OF YEARS, people have been practicing meditation for its positive benefits. While meditation is an old practice, only recently have science and technology begun to understand the positive benefits on the body and brain.

There have been numerous studies that show the practice of both meditation and mindfulness can have positive impacts, such as reducing stress, anxiety, and depression; increasing focus, creativity, happiness, health, among countless other benefits.

Everybody can benefit from a regular meditation practice, regardless of age or health status. Some recommended meditations apps and websites are listed here. There are many other resources, websites, and apps available, and different methods and styles may work for different people, so I encourage you to try these with others; you may find what works best for you.

Recommended Meditation and Mindfulness Apps

Buddhify 2

Buddhify 2 is an app with over eighty guided meditations for everyday life; these could be used when you have trouble sleeping, when you feel stressed, when you are traveling, or doing household chores.

Most are only a few minutes long and are quick and easy to get started, helping to bring mindfulness into your everyday life with little practice or knowledge of meditation and mindfulness. It's a one-off cost and is very cheap, with no ongoing monthly subscription fees.

This is an app that I use every week and recommend for beginners who don't have a lot of time or are unsure how to begin practicing meditation and mindfulness.

Headspace

Headspace is an app and website with ten-minute lessons on guided meditation.

This can be seen as a training course on how to learn how to meditate daily. There are ten lessons for free, with introductory videos explaining meditation and mindfulness that help understand how to stop your mind and thoughts from racing away and bring calm and a few minutes of peace into your day.

You can connect with your friends, and it has challenges to keep you meditating and encourage each other.

It's a paid monthly subscription; however, it contains a lot of value and content.

I use this app daily and highly recommend it if you want to develop a daily meditation habit and need guidance and lessons on how to start.

Calm

Calm is similar to Headspace in that they have both an app and website and offer guided meditation sessions.

Calm also has unguided meditation, with sounds of nature you can listen to while meditating. They have lessons on mindfulness, focus, and gratitude as well.

You can adjust the length of time you want to meditate, and they have short two-minute meditations to calm your mind and take a couple of minutes to relax without committing to a longer meditation session. This is a great way to start to make meditation a daily habit, no matter how busy you are.

As Headspace and Calm are similar, what works for you from these apps is a personal preference. Some people prefer Headspace, while others prefer Calm.

They both offer free lessons, so it's worth trying the free classes and seeing what works best for you and the style you prefer.

This is another app and website I use daily and highly recommend for people who are just starting to learn meditation and want to make it a daily habit.

Smiling Mind

Smiling Mind is free as an app and a website, run by a nonprofit organization. It teaches mindfulness and meditation training and has a range of lessons to build a meditation habit and have more mindfulness in your day.

They state that their mission is to provide accessible, life-long tools for mindfulness meditation to help reduce stress, pressure, the challenges of everyday life, and build happier and healthier people.

The website and app are very easy to use and have great stats and a dashboard to track your progress and motivate you to meditate regularly.

Their mindfulness meditation programs have been code-veloped with experts in the brain, health, and psychology. Being a free website and app, it is available to everyone around the world without cost.

Smiling Mind also offers meditation lessons for children and teenagers, as well as adults, so the meditation and mindfulness lessons are more structured and specific towards age groups compared to others.

The Smiling Mind program was created with an Australian accent. Some people have noted in the reviews that they find this difficult, as they're not used to the accent. I found the voice to be calming and didn't find this to be an issue. Different people find different accents more calming and easier to understand, so it's important to find a program that works for you.

Smiling Mind is great for getting started and turning meditation into a daily habit and practice. This is worth trying, as it's free and has a lot of value.

I use Smiling Mind and recommend it. However, I'm new to using it, so I haven't used it as much as Calm, Headspace, and Buddhify.

Stop Breathe Think

Stop Breathe Think is another meditation and mindfulness app and website that is also run by a nonprofit organization called Tools For Peace that aims to inspire people of all ages to develop kindness and compassion through mindfulness and meditation.

The content and guided sessions are free. The website and app are both well-presented and easy to navigate and use.

You can track your mood before and after meditating, and it has a great section to track your progress, the number of minutes you meditated, the number of days in a row you meditated, along with rewards and encouragement as you progress.

The length of the guided meditation sessions can be selected, so you can do a short meditation session when you are just getting started or feel like you don't have the time for a longer session. The guided meditation is narrated by one of the founders, along with musician KD Lang.

Stop Breathe Think aims to help you take a few minutes each day to experience calm in your life. It can be used for one-off meditations or to follow through the sessions to develop a daily meditation habit.

It has recommendations based on your mood. If you are feeling anxious or stressed, it will recommend different meditation sessions. It will also make a recommendation if you are feeling unhappy or can't sleep. Having meditations based on your mood and mindset is a great feature that will allow you to develop the practice of meditation to calm your thoughts or help your mood and mindset when you need it.

I also use Stop Breathe Think and recommend it.

1 Giant Mind

1 Giant Mind is also free and run by a nonprofit organization. It is only an app and is not available through the website. It is an app that teaches an introductory course in mediation to help make it a daily habit.

1 Giant Mind states that the app and method are easy to use and take minimal effort to implement and practice. They're intended for people with busy lives to help calm their busy minds. The app does not require concentration, focus, control, or adopting a belief system. The app and method are also set up so you can practice anywhere you can sit comfortably with your eyes closed for any amount of time.

1 Giant Mind is popular. It is free, and other people have highly recommended it. I have used it, however, and I had issues with the Android app; it never saved my progress, so I was unable to move forward in the lessons. I enjoyed the sessions I did. It isn't my first recommendation, but this is only due to the app issues I had when using it.

If the cost of the other websites/apps, such as Calm and Headspace, is too much, then this is certainly worth using to start a daily meditation habit.

The Mindfulness App

The Mindfulness app is another popular app for mindfulness and meditation. It is available as an app only, not via a website.

There is no subscription fee for the app; it's only a one-off purchase cost, so it's very affordable.

You can set how long you want to meditate, and you can

select whether to have a guided meditation or meditate in silence with the light ringing of a bell at different intervals during the meditation.

You can also set reminders to remind you to meditate at certain times of the day. This can be helpful in building a meditation habit each day, and you can also set reminders to check whether you are being mindful and remind you to be in the moment.

This app also has a statistics section, keeping track of your meditation and how it is progressing over time.

I have downloaded this app and tested it, but I have not used it on a regular basis. However, it comes recommended and is very popular, receiving high ratings for the app on the Apple App Store and Google Play Store.

Omvana

Omvana is available on the web and as an app. It provides a range of tracks for meditation, mindfulness, and other motivational and inspirational topics, such as the law of attraction, quitting bad habits, getting better sleep, and more.

The free account provides access to twenty-five tracks; however, to access the full range of tracks requires a monthly subscription cost.

There is background music for each guided track, and this can be customized and changed so you can match the guided meditation voice with a different background music track that suits you.

Omvana is the number-one selling health and fitness app in many countries around the world.

I have signed up and tried it, but I have never used it

other than testing it. However, given its popularity around the world, it works very well for many people.

Meditation and Mindfulness for Children

Smiling Mind

Smiling Mind offers meditations for children through the website and app. It is a great way for children to build a meditation habit to help them concentrate better in school and have more focus.

This is especially useful for kids today in the fast-paced, instant gratification world, where they are constantly bombarded with information that can be overwhelming and which can make it difficult to focus on study or learning for long periods of time, without getting restless and wanting to watch TV or play video games.

There are action-based tools that will guide the children through mindfulness meditation practices.

Meditation and Mindfulness for Teens/Young Adults

Smiling Mind

Along with lessons for adults and children, Smiling Mind also offers meditation and mindfulness lessons for teenagers/ young adults, where the lessons are structured around issues and stresses teens may face in their daily lives, which are very different from the stresses of adults or children.

Stop, Breathe, and Think

Stop Breathe Think provides practical methods of

mindfulness and meditation training through the website and app along with in-school programs and camps for young people.

They work with a range of schools, universities, and other organizations to help young people develop focus, mindfulness, happiness, and a positive mindset to help with the stresses of school and everyday life

Insight Timer

Insight Timer is a free mobile app with a focus on community and connecting with friends to meditate together and encourage each other to meditate. It has stats and milestones for tracking your progress.

I haven't used this app, but it is one of the top free meditation apps in the world. It seems focused more towards younger people or people interested in the community and friend aspects, which can be a great way to build a meditation habit, with accountability and friends to meditate and join with you.

MindShift

MindShift is a free app developed by a nonprofit organization, focused on anxiety disorders in collaboration with British Columbia Children's Hospital.

The app aims to help teens and young adults learn how to relax, develop more helpful ways of thinking, and help cope with and find ways to deal with anxiety.

This app has strategies for coping with everyday anxiety, as well as tools specifically for:

- Sleep
- Dealing with strong emotions

- Anxiety about school and tests
- Social anxiety
- Performance anxiety
- Perfectionism
- Worry
- Panic
- Conflict

CONCLUSION

Thank you, once again, for purchasing *Buddhism: Buddhism for Beginners: A Guide to Buddhist Teachings, Meditation, Mindfulness, and Inner Peace.*

I sincerely hope this material was useful to you through your discovery of Buddhism.

This is an introduction, and the teachings of Buddhism go much deeper than what is covered in this book.

There are a lot of resources in this book to continue your learning of Buddhism.

The next step would be to start with the meditation apps and resources referenced in this book and incorporate a small amount of meditation, mindfulness, and gratitude every day to start building these practices.

This book has included some quotes from the Buddha, the Dalai Lama, and Thich Nhat Hanh. Life is full of challenges, but these scholars have made the knowledge of

Buddhism and ways to overcome these challenges accessible to you in your everyday life. There are many writings, books, and quotes from these people that are worth reading to deepen your knowledge of Buddhism.

WHAT DID YOU THINK?

If you enjoyed this book, found issues, or want to get in contact:

If you appreciated the information provided in this book, please take a few moments to share your opinions and post a review on Amazon at the link here:

amazon.com/dp/B01NBC2I2S

I would be very grateful to you for your support if you found the information in the book useful.

If you have any feedback, found any errors in the book, or just want to get in contact to say hi, please feel free to email me at gshawbooks@gmail.com

Thank you for reading this book. Good luck in your spiritual journey and may you have peace and happiness in all areas of your life.

FREE BONUS GUIDES

FREE BONUS GUIDES ON MEDITATION AND MINDFULNESS

Get three free bonus guides to help you incorporate meditation and mindfulness into every day.

Guide 1: The Power of Meditation

Learn more about the power of meditation and how it can help you in your personal and professional life.

Guide 2: Stress Less

A guide to help reduce stress at home and work with meditation and mindfulness

Guide 3: The End to Multitasking

Learn how to get more done each day by avoiding multitasking and being more focused. This is a practical guide for work or study that includes focus exercises to improve mindfulness and increase focus and concentration.

Visit this link to get these free guides now:

wisefoxbooks.com/mindfulguide

FINAL MESSAGE

A final message from the Buddha:

"He who experiences the unity of life sees his own self in all beings, and all beings in his own self, and looks on everything with an impartial eye.

Hatred does not cease by hatred, but only by love; this is the eternal rule."

Printed in Poland
by Amazon Fulfillment
Poland Sp. z o.o., Wrocław

59921137R00061